AI-Powered Product Management

Essential Prompts for Every Stage

ETHAN DAWN HARPER

Copyright © 2024 Ethan Dawn Harper

All rights reserved. No part of this book may be reproduced, duplicated, or transmitted without the prior written permission from the author or the publisher.

Under no circumstances will any legal responsibility or blame be held against the publisher or author for any reparation, damages, or monetary loss due the information contained within this book, either directly or indirectly.

ISBN-13: 979-8-3235-23856

TABLE OF CONTENTS

Introduction v

Section 1: Product Management and Impact of AI. 9
    The Role of a Product Manager   10
    Key Skills and Competencies   10
    AI's Influence in Product Management   11
    Potential AI Tools for Product Managers   13
    The Importance of Effective AI Communication   16

Section 2: Market Analysis. 18
    Introduction to Market Analysis   19
    25 AI Prompts for Effective Market Analysis   20

Section 3: User Research 23
    Understanding User Need and Behavior   24
    25 AI Prompts for Conducting User Research   25

Section 4: Product Strategy. 28
    Crafting a Winning Product Strategy   29
    25 AI Prompts for Strategy Development   30

Section 5: Product Design 33
    Principles of Product Design   34
    25 AI Prompts. For Product Design   36

Section 6: Product Roadmapping. 38
    The Importance of Product Roadmaps   39
    25 AI Prompts for Product Roadmapping   40

Section 7: Agile and Scrum Techniques 43

    Agile Methodologies in Product Management 44

    25 AI Prompts for Agile and Scrum Management 46

Section 8: User Engagement and Retention 48

    Techniques of Increasing User Engagement 49

    25 AI Prompts for User Engagement and Retention 51

Section 9: Analytics and Data-Driven Decision-Making 53

    Leveraging Data in Product Management 54

    25 AI Prompts for Utilizing Analytics. 56

Section 10: Scaling Products. 58

    Strategies for Scaling Your Product 59

    25 AI Prompts for Product Scaling 61

Section 11: Product Launch and Marketing. 64

    Effective Product Launch Strategies. 65

    25 AI Prompts for Product lLaunch and Marketing 67

Section 12: Leadership and Stakeholder Management. 69

    Managing Teams and Stakeholders. 70

    25 AI Prompts for Leadership and Stakeholder Engagement 71

Conclusion 72

INTRODUCTION

In today's rapidly evolving digital landscape, the role of a product manager is more complex and demanding than ever before. With the advent of Artificial Intelligence (AI), new tools have emerged that can significantly enhance the decision-making processes and efficiency of product management. "*AI-Powered Product Management: Essential Prompts for Every Stage*" is designed to bridge the gap between traditional product management practices and the cutting-edge capabilities offered by AI. As product managers, the challenge is not only to manage and execute product development efficiently but also to innovate and stay ahead of market trends. AI offers powerful tools for achieving these goals, from deep data analysis to automated user insights. However, the potential of AI can be daunting due to its complexity and the breadth of its applications. This book demystifies the use of AI in product management by providing specific, actionable prompts that you can use to leverage AI technology in various aspects of your work.

Consider the example of predictive analytics in user behavior: by applying AI to understand and predict customer actions, product managers can proactively design features that cater to future needs, rather than merely reacting to user feedback. AI can also streamline the testing process, using algorithms to quickly identify potential flaws or areas for improvement, saving time and reducing costs significantly. In addition, AI-driven tools can automate routine tasks such as sorting through user feedback and prioritizing feature requests, allowing product managers to focus on strategic decision-making and product innovation. This not only improves productivity but also enhances the quality of the products developed.

Embracing AI in product management transforms traditional approaches, enabling more dynamic and responsive product development. AI facilitates a deeper understanding of market conditions and consumer behavior through advanced data analytics, allowing product managers to anticipate market demands and adjust strategies accordingly. This proactive approach is crucial in maintaining a competitive edge in a market where trends shift rapidly and consumer preferences evolve continuously.

Moreover, AI integration helps in managing the vast amount of data generated during the product life cycle. By utilizing machine learning algorithms, product managers can gain insights from data patterns that would be impossible to analyze manually. These insights can lead to the development of more personalized and effective products, ultimately increasing customer satisfaction and loyalty.

The effective use of AI also extends to enhancing customer interactions and improving overall user experience. For instance, chatbots and virtual assistants, powered by AI, can provide instant customer support and personalized communication at scale, which enriches the user experience and frees up human resources to tackle more complex problems.

However, to fully harness the potential of AI, product managers must also be aware of the ethical considerations and challenges associated with AI technologies, such as data privacy and algorithmic bias. It is essential to implement AI solutions responsibly, ensuring that they respect user privacy and provide equitable outcomes for all users.

In conclusion, "*AI-Powered Product Management: Essential Prompts for Every Stage*" equips product managers with the knowledge and tools needed to effectively integrate AI into their practices. By adopting AI, product managers can enhance their decision-making capabilities, optimize operational efficiency, and create innovative products that meet the evolving needs of their customers. As AI technology continues to advance, its role in product management will only grow, making it an indispensable element of modern product strategy.

How This Book Helps

Each chapter of this book is structured to offer a comprehensive look at a specific aspect of product management, followed by 25 tailored AI prompts that are directly applicable to that facet of managing products. The prompts are designed to be immediately actionable, helping you to implement AI tools and techniques in a structured and effective manner.

To get the most out of this book, start by reading through each chapter to understand the context and importance of the prompts provided. You can then apply these prompts directly to your current projects or use them as a training tool to improve your overall approach to AI in product management. Whether it's enhancing product customization, optimizing pricing strategies, or forecasting market trends, the AI prompts provided here can transform how you approach your role.

This book can serve as a reference guide—return to it whenever you need fresh ideas or specific guidance on using AI to solve complex product management challenges. By integrating AI into your daily operations, you will not only keep pace with technological advancements but also gain a competitive edge in the marketplace.

SECTION 1
UNDERSTANDING PRODUCT MANAGEMENT AND IMPACT OF AI

The Role of a Product Manager

Product management is a unique role that sits at the intersection of technology, business, and user experience. A product manager is essentially the CEO of the product, responsible for guiding the success of a product and leading the cross-functional team that is responsible for improving it. It is a role that balances strategic thinking with tactical execution.

Product managers set the vision and strategy for a product, defining what will be built and why it should be built. They are tasked with understanding market demands, potential opportunities, and customer needs. Once these elements are understood, product managers prioritize features, plan releases, and define the product roadmap, constantly iterating based on feedback and market changes.

Additionally, product managers must ensure alignment across various stakeholders including customers, business executives, and engineering teams. They negotiate and influence to maintain a cohesive direction, balancing diverse perspectives and sometimes conflicting interests. The success of a product often hinges on a product manager's ability to communicate effectively and rally a team around a shared vision.

Key Skills and Competencies

- *Strategic Thinking:* Ability to envision long-term product goals and the steps needed to get there. This includes understanding market trends, identifying customer needs, and anticipating competitive actions.

- *Analytical Skills:* Proficiency in using data to make informed decisions. This involves measuring product performance, analyzing customer feedback, and using data-driven insights to guide the development process.

- *Leadership and Communication:* Strong leadership skills are crucial as product managers must lead through influence. Excellent communication skills help in articulating the product vision, negotiating between different stakeholders, and ensuring team alignment.

- *Customer Focus:* A deep understanding of customer needs and the ability to empathize with users. This competency is essential for designing user-centric products that solve real problems.

- Technical Proficiency: While not always necessary, a good grasp of the technological aspects can help product managers communicate more effectively with engineering teams and make better decisions about what is feasible.

- *Project Management:* Organizational skills and the ability to manage timelines, resources, and personnel are important. Product managers must keep projects on track and handle multiple priorities simultaneously.

- *Adaptability:* The ability to pivot and adapt to changes swiftly. Product landscapes can change rapidly, and a successful product manager needs to be flexible in approach and mindset.

AI's Influence in Product Management

The integration of Artificial Intelligence (AI) into product management has fundamentally transformed the field, enhancing how product teams function and improving the precision of their outputs. AI's ability to swiftly process and analyze large datasets has significantly augmented decision-making processes and equipped product managers with predictive insights that were previously unattainable with traditional analytical methods. This capability enables a proactive approach to market changes and customer behaviors, facilitating a more dynamic and responsive product management strategy.

AI is revolutionizing traditional practices across several core areas:

Market Analysis: AI excels in identifying and interpreting market trends and consumer preferences at a granular level. Tools equipped with AI can monitor and analyze vast amounts of data from social media, web analytics, and other digital footprints, providing product managers with real-time insights into market dynamics. This helps in predicting market movements and effectively positioning products.

Customer Feedback Interpretation: AI technologies such as natural language processing (NLP) transform unstructured customer feedback from various channels into structured data that can be easily analyzed. This empowers product managers to identify common issues, gauge customer sentiment, and uncover underlying problems that may not be visible through manual analysis.

Product Lifecycle Management: AI can automate many aspects of product lifecycle management, from forecasting product demand to identifying the optimal times for product upgrades or discontinuations. Predictive analytics can foresee product performance across different stages of its lifecycle, allowing teams to make data-driven decisions on product iterations and enhancements.

Personalization and Customization: By analyzing individual user data, AI enables product teams to create highly personalized user experiences. This not only improves customer satisfaction but also boosts user engagement and loyalty by making products feel more tailored to individual needs.

Operational Efficiency: AI automates routine tasks such as data entry, report generation, and even some elements of project management, freeing up product managers to focus on strategic tasks. AI-driven automation helps in maintaining a lean operational process, reducing errors, and increasing overall team productivity.

The influence of AI in product management is not just about enhancing existing processes but also about opening new avenues for innovation and strategic thinking. By leveraging AI, product managers can not only anticipate and react to market needs more swiftly but can also drive the product development process towards more innovative and customer-centric solutions. This shift is not merely operational but strategic, placing AI at the heart of product management's future.

Potential AI Tools for Product Managers

Product managers can greatly benefit from a variety of AI tools and AI-integrated platforms designed to enhance decision-making, streamline operations, and gain deep market and customer insights. Here is a detailed overview of some of them:

AI-driven Market Research Tools:
- Crayon: An AI tool that actively monitors market changes and competitor activities, providing real-time insights that help product managers stay strategically ahead. It leverages AI to analyze data across various sources for comprehensive competitive intelligence.
- Pathmatics: An AI-supported tool that offers digital marketing intelligence by analyzing where and how competitors are advertising, utilizing AI to decode strategy and spending patterns.
-

Customer Feedback Analysis Tools:
- Chattermill: This tool uses deep learning, an AI technology, to analyze and aggregate customer feedback across multiple channels, helping product managers understand customer sentiments and preferences in depth.
- Medallia: An AI-integrated platform that captures and processes customer signals, using AI algorithms to predict customer behaviors and provide actionable insights for enhancing customer engagement.
-

Predictive Analytics Platforms:
- Gainsight: An AI-integrated platform that offers tools for customer success and product experience, using predictive analytics to foresee customer trends and customize user experiences.
- Pendo: Integrates AI to provide comprehensive analytics on user behavior and product usage, enhancing product management decisions through data-driven insights and automated feedback collection.

AI-based Project Management Tools:
- Forecast: A project management tool powered by AI,

designed to optimize team workflows and predict project timelines, helping manage resources and schedules more efficiently.

- Monday.com: While primarily a project management platform, it incorporates AI features to automate and optimize project tracking and resource allocation.

Automated Testing Tools:
- Testim: Uses AI, specifically machine learning, to create and maintain automated test scripts. This tool helps teams efficiently manage quality assurance by adapting to changes in the app during testing.
- Sealights: An AI tool that focuses on test automation effectiveness, using AI to optimize testing processes and ensure high-quality deployment in agile environments.

User Behavior Analytics Tools:
- Mixpanel: An analytics platform that employs AI to analyze detailed user interactions, allowing for precise measurement of how changes affect user behavior and product performance.
- Heap: Automatically captures user actions on digital platforms and uses AI to analyze impact, making it easier to understand user behavior and optimize product features.

AI-enhanced Business Intelligence Tools:
- Tableau: Integrates AI capabilities to provide more intuitive and predictive business intelligence insights, making data analysis accessible and actionable for strategic decisions.
- Looker (part of Google Cloud): A business intelligence tool that supports AI functionalities, enabling users to explore and share real-time analytics effortlessly, enhancing decision-making processes across the organization.

These AI tools and AI-integrated platforms are essential for product managers seeking to enhance their analytical capabilities, improve operational efficiency, and drive innovative product strategies tailored to evolving market and customer needs.

The Importance of Effective Communication with AI

In the era of AI-driven technology, mastering the art of communicating effectively with AI systems through well-structured prompts is crucial for product managers. This skill is essential not only for leveraging the full potential of AI in product management but also for ensuring the accuracy and efficiency of the insights generated.

Clear and precise communication with AI ensures that the system fully understands the tasks at hand, which significantly improves the relevance and accuracy of the outputs. Ambiguities or inaccuracies in communication can lead to misinterpretations by the AI, resulting in outputs that may be irrelevant or off-target. This precision in results is vital, as it directly impacts the effectiveness of decision-making processes and the strategic use of AI-driven insights.

Moreover, well-crafted prompts enhance operational efficiency by reducing the need for iterative cycles often required to refine AI outputs. This direct and effective communication saves valuable time and resources, allowing product teams to focus more on strategic initiatives rather than operational adjustments.

Effective communication also plays a critical role in the user experience, particularly for AI tools that interact directly with customers, such as chatbots or AI-driven customer service platforms. The quality of these interactions can significantly influence customer satisfaction and perception, making clear and user-friendly communication a key factor in maintaining high levels of customer engagement and satisfaction.

As organizations scale and the use of AI expands, the ability to communicate effectively with AI helps maintain the consistency and reliability of AI-generated insights. This scalability is crucial for organizations that rely on AI to support decision-making across various levels and departments.

Furthermore, understanding how to craft effective AI prompts encourages creativity and innovation among product managers. With a solid grasp of AI capabilities and communication strategies, managers are better positioned to explore innovative applications of AI, potentially leading to new product developments, market opportunities, and competitive advantages.

Lastly, proper communication is integral to managing the risks associated with automated decisions. By ensuring clarity and accuracy in the prompts used, product managers can mitigate potential errors that could lead to financial losses, reputational damage, or strategic missteps.

In conclusion, the ability to effectively communicate with AI is not merely a technical skill but a fundamental aspect of modern product management. It requires an ongoing commitment to learning and adapting to new AI advancements, as well as continuous practice in real-world applications. By focusing on developing these communication skills, product teams can maximize the benefits of AI integration and ensure their initiatives are both successful and sustainable.

SECTION 2

MARKET ANALYSIS

Introduction to Market Analysis

Market analysis is a cornerstone of effective product management. It equips product managers with the insights needed to make informed decisions about product development, positioning, and evolution. Through a comprehensive examination of the market, product managers gain a deep understanding of current trends, competitor actions, customer behaviors, and market needs.

This analysis involves examining the trajectory of market sectors, including technological advancements, economic factors, and shifts in consumer preferences. It also includes a thorough assessment of competitors, evaluating their products, market share, strengths, and weaknesses. Moreover, it looks at customer segmentation, which helps in identifying specific groups within the broader market and tailoring products to meet their unique needs.

Understanding market needs is crucial. It involves identifying what customers truly desire from products, which often includes analyzing customer feedback and data to pinpoint their primary challenges and expectations. This leads to identifying market opportunities—areas where existing solutions fall short and where new or improved products can make a significant impact.

The strategic value of market analysis lies in its ability to guide product strategy and innovation. By accurately interpreting market data, product managers can predict which product features or innovations will meet current and future demands. This reduces the risks associated with product development by ensuring that new products are both necessary and desired in the marketplace.

Furthermore, effective market analysis underpins strategic planning, helping product managers align their product vision with market realities. It also informs risk management, enabling proactive adjustments in response to potential market shifts. Effective allocation of resources based on market data ensures that investments are made into areas most likely to yield high returns, and targeted marketing strategies can be developed to reach the right audience efficiently.

In summary, market analysis is not just about understanding the market; it's about leveraging that understanding to make smarter, more strategic decisions that drive product success and innovation. This book will guide product managers on how to apply AI tools to enhance this essential function, providing specific, actionable prompts that streamline and strengthen the market analysis process.

25 AI Prompts for Effective Market Analysis

1. "Generate a market trend report for [industry] over the last year."
2. "Identify emerging technologies affecting the [specific product category]."
3. "Analyze competitor product launches in [market] during the last six months."
4. "Summarize customer reviews of [competitor's product] for sentiment analysis."
5. "Forecast the next quarter's market demand for [product category]."
6. "Evaluate the effectiveness of pricing strategies across [specific industry]."

7. "Create a SWOT analysis for [your product] in the current market environment."
8. "Detect market gaps and opportunities for [product line] in [target market]."
9. "Profile top three competitors in [market segment] based on market share and growth."
10. "Conduct a feature comparison of leading products in [product category]."
11. "Assess customer demographics for [product category] using social media data analysis."
12. "Map out customer journey for purchasing [type of product] online."
13. "Analyze regulatory impact on [product line] in [specific regions]."
14. "Predict changes in consumer behavior in response to [economic event]."
15. "Generate a report on how seasonal trends affect sales of [product]."
16. "Identify key drivers of customer satisfaction in [industry]."
17. "Estimate the market penetration of [product type] in [target market] over time."
18. "Determine the most effective marketing channels for [specific product]."
19. "Calculate the lifetime value of customers acquiring [product] through online platforms."
20. "Investigate the impact of international trade policies on [product category]."
21. "Track the adoption rate of new features introduced in [last product update]."
22. "Assess the viability of entering a new market with [product]."
23. "Create a risk analysis for potential market entry barriers

for [new product]."

24. "Examine the influence of cultural factors on product acceptance in [new market]."

25. "Evaluate the competitive landscape after [recent industry disruption]."

SECTION 3

USER RESEARCH

Understanding User Needs and Behaviors

User research is crucial to the success of any product as it directly influences every aspect of product development and lifecycle management. At its core, user research is about deeply understanding who the users are—diving into their behaviors, needs, preferences, and frustrations—to directly inform the design, functionality, and enhancements of a product. By aligning product features with the actual requirements of users, companies can ensure greater satisfaction and sustained user engagement.

The process of user research utilizes a variety of methods to gather and analyze data, providing a comprehensive understanding of user interactions with the product. These methods include:

- *Surveys and Questionnaires:* Good for quantitative data and broad feedback.
- *Interviews:* Offer qualitative insights from individual users.
- Focus Groups: Allow for discussion among users, uncovering deeper insights.
- *Usability Testing:* Observes users interacting with your product to identify usability issues.
- *Ethnographic Research:* Involves observing users in their natural environment.
- *Card Sorting:* Helps understand how users categorize information.
- *A/B Testing:* Compares two versions of a product to see which performs better.

Effective user research does more than just align product

features with user needs; it forms the basis for strategic decision-making that can significantly enhance product success. Understanding user behaviors and needs helps product managers:

- *Prioritize Feature Development:* Insights from user research help in prioritizing the development of features that users care about most, ensuring efficient use of resources.
- *Enhance User Satisfaction:* By designing and refining features based on user feedback, products become more user-friendly and relevant, enhancing user satisfaction and loyalty.
- *Reduce Risk:* Understanding what users need and value can significantly reduce the risk associated with new product features or entirely new products as decisions are based on validated user data.
- *Drive Innovation:* User research often uncovers latent needs and pain points, providing opportunities for innovation and differentiation in crowded markets.

This data-driven approach allows product managers to make informed decisions that not only improve the existing user experience but also anticipate future needs, thereby driving product success and ensuring long-term viability in the marketplace. Through comprehensive and continuous user research, product teams can stay aligned with their users' evolving expectations and maintain a competitive edge in delivering superior user experiences.

25 AI Prompts for Conducting User Research

Data Collection:
1. "Generate user personas for our target demographic based on recent interaction data."

2. "Map out the typical user journey for customers purchasing [product category]."
3. "Create a report on user behavior patterns for [product] using web analytics data."
4. "Profile user interactions within the app to identify potential drop-off points."
5. "Extract actionable insights from user session recordings to improve [product interface]."
6. "Identify unmet user needs by analyzing queries and requests submitted through customer support."
7. "Analyze cross-platform usage data to understand device preferences among our users."

Analysis:
1. "Analyze user satisfaction trends from the past year's survey data for [product name]."
2. "Summarize customer feedback on [specific feature] to identify common themes."
3. "Identify the top user complaints from online reviews over the last three months."
4. "Conduct a sentiment analysis on social media mentions related to [product] this quarter."
5. "Analyze demographic data to tailor [product] features to user preferences in [market segment]."
6. "Investigate patterns in feature usage to identify opportunities for product cross-selling."
7. "Conduct a comparative analysis of user satisfaction across different product lines."

Prediction and Forecasting
1. "Predict how changes to [product feature] might impact user satisfaction."
2. "Forecast the adoption rate of [upcoming feature] among our

existing user base."
3. "Generate insights on how external factors (e.g., economic, seasonal) influence user behavior."
4. "Generate a predictive model to determine future user needs based on current trends."

User Testing and Evaluation
1. "Evaluate the usability of [new product feature] through automated user testing simulations."
2. "Compare user engagement metrics before and after the recent product update."
3. "Measure the impact of recent changes in [product] on user retention rates."
4. "Determine the effectiveness of the current onboarding process for new users."
5. "Assess the correlation between customer service interactions and user satisfaction levels."
6. "Evaluate the impact of pricing adjustments on user purchase behavior."
7. "Segment users based on usage frequency and generate tailored engagement strategies."

SECTION 4

PRODUCT STRATEGY

Crafting a Winning Product Strategy

Creating a successful product strategy is about much more than merely deciding features and timelines; it involves a holistic vision that guides a product from conception through its market lifecycle. This process begins with a deep understanding of the market and customer insights, which are crucial for identifying target demographics, understanding their needs, and pinpointing the specific problems the product aims to solve. Awareness of market trends and customer behaviors is also essential to ensure the product remains relevant and competitive.

A thorough competitive analysis helps delineate where the product fits within the market landscape, identifying opportunities for differentiation and understanding competitor strengths and weaknesses. The product strategy must clearly articulate the product vision—what the product aspires to achieve in the long term and how it supports the broader company strategy. This vision ties directly into product positioning, which defines how the product will be perceived in the market and what makes it unique.

The practical application of a product strategy is realized through a detailed product roadmap that outlines how the product will evolve over time. It shows planned features and versions aligned with strategic objectives, market needs, and company goals. Prioritizing features is a critical component of this roadmap, as it determines resource allocation to maximize impact on customer satisfaction and business outcomes.

The strategy should also clearly define the business model, outlining how the company will generate revenue from the product. This includes setting a pricing strategy and deciding on a revenue model, such as subscriptions, one-time purchases, or a freemium model. An effective go-to-market strategy is also vital, encompassing marketing and sales strategies, distribution channels, and customer support plans to ensure a successful product launch and sustained market presence.

Moreover, the strategy must incorporate performance metrics to measure success and guide future decisions. These key performance indicators help track progress against goals, adapting the strategy as needed based on performance data.

Finally, leveraging AI can greatly enhance strategic planning. AI tools offer deeper data analysis, enable predictive modeling of market trends, and help personalize customer experiences. They can simulate different market scenarios, optimize pricing strategies, and predict customer behaviors, which are invaluable for refining a product strategy to not only meet current market needs but also adapt to future changes.

In essence, crafting a winning product strategy is about integrating all these elements into a coherent plan that drives the product's development, launch, and growth in alignment with both market opportunities and company objectives.

25 AI Prompts for Strategy Development

1. "Generate a long-term roadmap for [product] based on current market trends and technology advancements."
2. "Analyze competitive positioning for [product] within its category and suggest strategic adjustments."
3. "Forecast the potential market size and growth for [new product idea] over the next five years."

4. "Identify key differentiation points of [product] compared to main competitors."
5. "Suggest optimal pricing strategy for [product] based on competitor pricing and customer value perception."
6. "Evaluate the impact of recent industry changes on the product lifecycle of [product]."
7. "Assess customer segments that are most likely to convert for [new product feature]."
8. "Create scenarios for future market developments and how they could affect [product line]."
9. "Recommend marketing channels that will maximize reach and engagement for [target demographic]."
10. "Determine the feasibility of introducing [product] into a new geographic market."
11. "Simulate customer response to potential new features or services for [product]."
12. "Develop a strategy for customer retention based on analysis of user behavior data."
13. "Identify potential partnerships or collaborations that could enhance product offering."
14. "Propose a bundle strategy for [product family] to increase customer lifetime value."
15. "Assess the viability of a freemium versus premium model for [software product]."
16. "Analyze the effectiveness of past promotional campaigns and suggest improvements."
17. "Explore the impact of regulatory changes on product development and market entry."
18. "Recommend adjustments to product features based on user feedback and usability testing."
19. "Predict the impact of economic shifts on product sales and suggest mitigation strategies."
20. "Evaluate the scalability of [product line] to handle increased

market demand."
21. "Generate user personas for new market segments targeted by [upcoming product]."
22. "Conduct a risk analysis for potential new features or market expansions."
23. "Plan a phased rollout for [new product] including pilot testing and full market launch."
24. "Recommend resource allocation for product development based on strategic priorities."
25. "Analyze cross-selling opportunities within the existing product portfolio."

SECTION 5

PRODUCT DESIGN

Principles of Product Design

Product design is a critical endeavor that melds the arts and sciences, involving a deep understanding of aesthetics, functionality, usability, and technology to create products that resonate with users and succeed in the market. The essence of good product design lies in its ability to solve real problems in intuitive and innovative ways while ensuring the product is appealing and easy to use.

At the core of product design is the principle of User-Centered Design (UCD), which places the user at the forefront throughout the design process. This approach ensures that every design decision—from the initial concept to the final product—addresses the users' needs and feedback. It involves extensive user research, iterative testing, and continuous refinement based on real-world use. This not only enhances the usability of the product but also ensures it meets the functional requirements of its intended audience.

Simplicity and clarity are paramount in product design. The goal is to make complex systems understandable and manageable for the user. This means designing interfaces and experiences that are straightforward, with clear navigation paths and minimalistic design that enhances user interaction without overwhelming them. Consistency across the product's interface reinforces this simplicity, aiding in user learning and improving the overall user experience by making interactions predictable and reliable.

Accessibility is another fundamental principle, ensuring that products are usable by people of all abilities, including those with disabilities. This involves designing with considerations for diverse user needs, such as adjustable text sizes, high contrast visuals, and support for assistive technologies. By embracing accessibility, products can reach a wider audience and provide a more inclusive user experience.

The emotional connection a product fosters with its users can significantly impact its success. This involves leveraging design to evoke positive feelings and emotions, making the product not only functional but also enjoyable to use. Emotional design can lead to greater user engagement and loyalty, as users often gravitate towards products that they feel a personal connection with.

In the modern context, sustainability has become increasingly important in product design. Designers are now looking to reduce environmental impact by selecting eco-friendly materials and designing for longevity and recyclability. Sustainable design practices not only appeal to environmentally conscious consumers but also contribute to a broader commitment to global sustainability.

Finally, innovation and flexibility are essential in keeping up with the fast pace of technological and market changes. Successful product design involves a willingness to explore new ideas and adapt to feedback and changing conditions. This dynamic approach helps ensure that the product remains relevant and continues to meet user needs over time.

These principles are often executed through Design Thinking, a methodology that emphasizes empathy with the users, a thorough understanding of their needs, and continuous iteration. This process encourages innovative solutions that are desirable from a user perspective, technically feasible, and commercially viable.

25 AI Prompts for Design and Development Phases

1. "Generate initial design concepts based on user preferences for [product]."
2. "Simulate interactions with prototype features of [product] to identify usability issues."
3. "Optimize the user interface layout of [product] using machine learning."
4. "Analyze feedback on prototypes of [product] to prioritize feature development."
5. "Predict how design changes in [product] will affect user satisfaction and engagement."
6. "Automate testing of user paths in [product] to ensure intuitive navigation."
7. "Evaluate the impact of different color schemes on user sentiment for [product]."
8. "Test virtual prototypes of [product] in varied user environments using AI."
9. "Optimize performance of [product] through analysis of beta test data."
10. "Create detailed user scenarios for testing new features of [product]."
11. "Automatically generate code for new features of [product]."
12. "Simulate ergonomic design analysis for [physical product] using AI."
13. "Forecast performance of [product] hardware under different usage scenarios."
14. "Refine voice user interfaces of [product] using natural language processing."
15. "Refine security features of [product] through continuous AI-driven testing."

16. "Assess environmental impact of [product] materials using AI analytics."
17. "Visualize [product] designs in augmented reality for enhanced presentations."
18. "Automatically create user documentation based on design specifications of [product]."
19. "Monitor product quality during pilot runs of [product] using AI tools."
20. "Facilitate real-time collaboration for [product] design teams globally using AI."
21. "Optimize supply chain decisions for [product] components using predictive analytics."
22. "Enhance integration testing for features of [product] under real-world conditions using AI."
23. "Generate automated responses to user queries during [product] beta testing."
24. "Predict maintenance and support challenges for [product] with AI durability testing."
25. "Analyze features of competitive products and provide insights for enhancing [product]."

SECTION 6

PRODUCT ROADMAPPING

The Importance of Product Roadmaps

A product roadmap is a strategic tool that charts the course of a product over time, integrating vision, direction, and planned milestones. It serves as a visual communication device that helps teams understand where the product is headed and the steps necessary to get there. By providing a clear outline of priorities and timelines, the roadmap aligns the organization's efforts around a shared goal, ensuring that everyone from development teams to stakeholders understands their roles in the product's journey.

Creating a product roadmap starts with defining the strategic goals of the product, which are derived from broader business objectives and market opportunities. This involves identifying key features, enhancements, and innovations that will deliver value to customers while supporting the company's overall strategy. Each element on the roadmap is prioritized based on its impact, the resources required, and its alignment with other business activities.

A well-crafted roadmap not only outlines what the product teams will deliver but also highlights the why behind each decision. This clarity is crucial for maintaining focus and motivation, particularly when teams need to navigate through complex product challenges or when prioritizing competing interests. It also facilitates better stakeholder communication, providing a framework for discussing progress, negotiating resources, and setting realistic expectations.

Effective roadmapping also requires flexibility. Markets can change rapidly, new technologies can emerge, and customer preferences can shift. A dynamic roadmap allows teams to adapt their plans based on these changes, incorporating new data and feedback without losing sight of the overall product strategy. This adaptability is essential for staying relevant and competitive in fast-paced industries.

In addition to aligning and guiding internal teams, roadmaps can also build confidence among external stakeholders, including investors, partners, and customers. By transparently sharing the product's direction and progress, companies can foster trust and secure buy-in from these critical audiences. The roadmap essentially acts as a commitment to the product's future, demonstrating that the company is invested in continuous improvement and responsive to user needs.

Furthermore, the process of roadmapping itself encourages strategic thinking and collaboration. It prompts discussions about market trends, technological advancements, and business goals, driving a deeper understanding of how the product can evolve to meet the needs of tomorrow. It also provides an opportunity for various departments to input their unique perspectives, ensuring that the roadmap reflects a comprehensive approach to product development.

Ultimately, the product roadmap is more than just a document or a tool; it's a strategic asset that guides the entire lifecycle of the product. It helps teams navigate the complexities of product development, from conception through release and beyond, ensuring that each step is purposeful and aligned with a larger vision.

25 AI Prompts for Effective Roadmapping

1. "Generate a timeline for upcoming feature releases based

on current development velocity."
2. "Analyze historical data to predict potential delays in the product roadmap milestones."
3. "Map dependencies between planned features to optimize the development sequence."
4. "Assess the impact of market changes on the current product roadmap and suggest adjustments."
5. "Identify resource gaps that could affect the planned roadmap and recommend solutions."
6. "Forecast the ROI for each major feature or milestone in the product roadmap."
7. "Evaluate customer feedback to prioritize features in the next roadmap update."
8. "Simulate different roadmap scenarios to determine the optimal path for product development."
9. "Create visual representations of the product roadmap for stakeholder presentations."
10. "Recommend strategic partnerships based on alignment with roadmap goals and timelines."
11. "Analyze competitor roadmaps to identify trends and opportunities for differentiation."
12. "Generate alerts for upcoming deadlines and critical milestones."
13. "Provide a risk assessment for each stage of the product roadmap."
14. "Track and report on progress against roadmap objectives in real-time."
15. "Use data analytics to refine the estimation accuracy of roadmap timelines."
16. "Suggest feature adjustments based on emerging technologies that could impact the roadmap."
17. "Predict customer demand for planned features to validate roadmap decisions."

18. "Identify potential legal or regulatory issues that could impact roadmap execution."
19. "Recommend adjustments to the roadmap based on new business priorities or goals."
20. "Assess the scalability of the product infrastructure to support the roadmap's long-term goals."
21. "Evaluate the effectiveness of previous roadmap phases to improve future planning."
22. "Generate a breakdown of budget allocation for each phase of the roadmap."
23. "Simulate the impact of external economic factors on the product roadmap."
24. "Provide strategic insights for phase transitions in the product lifecycle within the roadmap."
25. "Recommend communication strategies to keep all stakeholders aligned with the roadmap."

SECTION 7

AGILE AND SCRUM TECHNIQUES

Agile Methodologies in Product Management

Agile methodologies have revolutionized product management by introducing flexibility, continuous improvement, and a strong emphasis on customer feedback into the product development process. Originally designed for software development, the principles of Agile have transcended industry boundaries, enabling teams in various sectors to adapt swiftly to changes, optimize collaboration, and enhance product relevance and quality through iterative cycles.

The essence of Agile in product management lies in its iterative development approach. Projects are broken down into manageable units known as sprints, each typically lasting a few weeks and culminating in a usable product increment. This process allows teams to incorporate feedback continuously and make adjustments in real time, ensuring the product evolves in line with user needs and market demands.

Agile fosters a customer-centric approach by embedding customer feedback loops into every phase of the product lifecycle. Regular interaction with customers and stakeholders ensures that the product direction is aligned with user expectations and business objectives, thereby increasing the likelihood of market success and customer satisfaction.

In Agile environments, cross-functional teams collaborate closely. Members from diverse functions—such as design, development, marketing, and customer support—work together in self-organizing teams. This setup enhances decision-making efficiency and fosters a creative problem-solving environment where innovation thrives.

Transparency and communication are pivotal in Agile methodologies. Daily stand-ups and regular sprint reviews keep everyone informed about project progress, challenges, and next steps. This high level of communication ensures that issues are addressed promptly and that the project remains on track toward its strategic goals.

Moreover, Agile emphasizes quality throughout the development process. Continuous integration and regular testing ensure that each product increment is functional and meets quality standards. This ongoing attention to quality reduces risks and eliminates the need for extensive revisions at later stages.

Agile also advocates for sustainable development practices, promoting a balanced workload that prevents burnout and maintains high productivity over time. This approach not only supports the well-being of the team but also ensures consistent progress without the disruptions commonly associated with deadline-driven crunch times.

The adoption of Agile methodologies brings substantial benefits, including faster time to market, increased flexibility to adapt to feedback and changes, higher customer satisfaction through continuous engagement, and improved risk management by identifying and addressing issues early in the development process.

Overall, Agile methodologies transform the landscape of product management by embedding a proactive, responsive, and user-focused approach into the fabric of product development. This methodology ensures that products not only meet but exceed user expectations while remaining adaptable in the face of evolving market conditions.

25 AI Prompts for Agile and Scrum Management

1. "Generate a list of user stories from customer feedback for the next sprint."
2. "Simulate sprint outcomes based on different team velocity scenarios."
3. "Analyze burn down charts to identify potential bottlenecks in the current sprint."
4. "Predict the impact of backlog changes on the sprint timeline."
5. "Suggest improvements for Scrum ceremonies based on team feedback analysis."
6. "Calculate the optimal sprint length based on historical performance data."
7. "Identify key factors influencing sprint success from past projects."
8. "Recommend tasks prioritization in the backlog for the upcoming sprint."
9. "Evaluate the effectiveness of the daily stand-up structure and propose modifications."
10. "Assess the alignment of sprint goals with overarching product strategy."
11. "Forecast resource needs for future sprints using predictive analytics."
12. "Determine risk levels for each item in the product backlog."
13. "Create a dashboard to visualize sprint progress in real-time."
14. "Generate automated sprint reports summarizing achievements and areas for improvement."
15. "Provide data-driven suggestions for enhancing cross-functional collaboration."

16. "Analyze the impact of external factors on sprint planning and execution."
17. "Optimize the product backlog with machine learning to prioritize user value."
18. "Simulate customer response to prototype features developed in the sprint."
19. "Measure team morale and its impact on sprint productivity."
20. "Propose adjustments to the Scrum framework to better suit project specifics."
21. "Analyze historical sprint data to predict future challenges and successes."
22. "Suggest evidence-based strategies to improve Scrum Master effectiveness."
23. "Evaluate the scalability of Agile practices within the organization."
24. "Develop predictive models to estimate feature completion times accurately."
25. "Assess the contribution of each sprint to the overall product roadmap."

SECTION 8

USER ENGAGEMENT AND RETENTION

Techniques for Increasing User Engagement

Increasing user engagement is essential for the success of any product, as it directly influences customer satisfaction, retention, and ultimately, the longevity of the product in the market. Engaging users involves not only attracting them to the product but also encouraging continuous interaction that enhances their overall experience.

To effectively increase user engagement, it's crucial to first deeply understand user behaviors, preferences, and needs. This understanding can be achieved through meticulous analysis of user interaction data, direct feedback, and observing how users interact with the product in various contexts. By leveraging this data, product managers can identify what users value most in the product and where there may be barriers to engagement.

Personalization plays a significant role in boosting user engagement. Tailoring the user experience to individual preferences and behaviors can make users feel valued and understood, thereby increasing their connection to the product. Personalization can range from customized content and personalized product recommendations to individualized user interfaces.

Interactive elements also greatly enhance engagement by making the user experience more dynamic and enjoyable. Features like interactive tutorials, in-app games, or engaging questionnaires can transform passive usage into active participation. Gamification is another powerful tool, incorporating elements of game playing such as point scoring, competition with others, or rules of play, to increase user activity and loyalty.

Communication is key to maintaining and increasing engagement. Regular updates about new features, tips on product usage, or upcoming events keep users informed and involved. Notifications should be optimized to catch users' attention at the right times without becoming intrusive.

Community building also significantly contributes to user engagement. Creating a space where users can interact with each other, share their experiences, and provide mutual support can foster a strong sense of community and attachment to the product. Whether through social media, forums, or built-in community features within the product, these interactions can transform individual user experiences into collective engagement.

Moreover, continuous improvement based on user feedback is vital. Users are more likely to stay engaged with a product they feel is evolving in response to their feedback. Implementing changes that users want to see not only improves the product but also deepens users' investment in the product's future.

Finally, analyzing the effectiveness of engagement strategies is crucial for sustained improvement. Regularly testing different approaches allows teams to understand what works and what doesn't, enabling them to fine-tune their strategies. Tools and metrics such as engagement rates, session lengths, and user retention rates provide valuable insights into how well users are interacting with the product over time.

By implementing these techniques, product managers can create a more engaging product experience that resonates with users and encourages long-term engagement. This not only boosts the immediate appeal of the product but also builds a foundation for lasting user relationships and ongoing product success.

25 AI Prompts for User Engagement and Retention

1. "Analyze patterns in user activity to identify the most engaging features of the product."
2. "Generate personalized content recommendations for users based on their browsing history."
3. "Simulate the impact of different user engagement strategies on overall retention rates."
4. "Predict which users are at risk of churning and suggest targeted engagement strategies."
5. "Evaluate the effectiveness of current loyalty programs in enhancing user retention."
6. "Identify optimal times for sending push notifications to maximize user engagement."
7. "Analyze user feedback to identify potential improvements that could enhance user satisfaction."
8. "Recommend changes to the user interface that could improve usability and engagement."
9. "Create a user segmentation model to tailor engagement strategies to different user groups."
10. "Assess the impact of new features on user retention and engagement through A/B testing."
11. "Forecast the long-term engagement trends based on current data analytics."
12. "Develop predictive models to estimate the lifetime value of engaged users."
13. "Optimize in-app messaging to increase user interaction and engagement."
14. "Evaluate the response to social media campaigns and their

effect on user engagement."
15. "Suggest new gamification elements to introduce based on user demographics."
16. "Analyze the drop-off points in the user journey where users typically disengage."
17. "Propose automated support solutions to improve user satisfaction and retention."
18. "Examine the correlation between update frequency and user retention rates."
19. "Generate insights into user preferences for customization options in the product."
20. "Identify key drivers of user satisfaction and loyalty from historical data."
21. "Recommend best practices for community management to foster a sense of belonging."
22. "Assess the usability of mobile versus desktop interfaces in retaining users."
23. "Explore the effectiveness of referral programs in boosting user engagement."
24. "Determine the impact of pricing changes on user retention and engagement."
25. "Analyze competitor engagement strategies and their success rates for benchmarking."

SECTION 9

ANALYTICS AND DATA-DRIVEN DECISION MAKING

Leveraging Data in Product Management

In the realm of product management, data acts as a foundational element that informs and drives decision-making processes. The ability to effectively gather, analyze, and act upon data can significantly distinguish successful products from those that struggle to find market relevance. By leveraging data, product managers can gain a deeper understanding of the market, refine product features, enhance user experiences, and ultimately drive business growth.

The process of leveraging data in product management starts with data collection. This involves gathering information from a variety of sources such as user interactions, digital footprints, sales transactions, market research, and customer feedback. The advent of big data technologies has enabled the capture and storage of vast amounts of data, providing a rich resource for gaining insights into user behavior and market trends.

Once data is collected, the next step is data analysis. This is where analytical tools and techniques come into play, transforming raw data into actionable insights. Product managers use quantitative methods like statistical analysis, data mining, and machine learning to identify patterns, trends, and correlations. For example, data analysis can reveal which product features are most used, which are underperforming, and how different user segments interact with the product.

Predictive analytics is another powerful tool at the disposal of product managers. By modeling data from past behaviors, product managers can forecast future trends, user actions, and market dynamics. This predictive capability allows them to anticipate market needs, adapt strategies proactively, and stay ahead of the competition. For instance, predicting seasonal spikes in product usage can help in planning marketing campaigns or optimizing inventory levels.

Segmentation analysis is crucial for personalizing marketing efforts and product development. By segmenting the user base into distinct groups based on shared characteristics or behaviors, product managers can tailor product offerings to better meet the needs of each segment. This targeted approach not only improves user satisfaction but also increases the effectiveness of marketing strategies.

Data-driven decision-making extends beyond product features and marketing. It also encompasses strategic decisions about pricing, distribution, and customer support. Data can indicate the most profitable price points, the most effective distribution channels, and the most common customer issues needing support. This holistic approach ensures that all aspects of product management are optimized for market success.

Moreover, continuous monitoring and real-time data analysis enable product managers to react quickly to changes in user behavior or market conditions. Real-time dashboards can provide ongoing insights into product performance, alerting managers to potential issues before they become critical problems.

Ultimately, leveraging data empowers product managers to make informed decisions that are backed by empirical evidence rather than intuition alone. It ensures that resources are allocated efficiently, risks are managed effectively, and product strategies are aligned with actual market and user needs. In an increasingly competitive and dynamic market, the ability to effectively leverage data can be a significant competitive advantage, driving innovation and ensuring long-term success.

25 AI Prompts for Utilizing Analytics

Here are AI-driven prompts that can help product managers utilize analytics for data-driven decision making:

1. "Generate predictive models to forecast user growth and product adoption."
2. "Analyze user behavior data to identify common paths through the product."
3. "Create segmentation analysis to determine the most valuable customer groups."
4. "Evaluate the effectiveness of different marketing channels in driving user engagement."
5. "Perform cohort analysis to understand user retention over specific periods."
6. "Calculate the lifetime value of customers acquired through various channels."
7. "Identify patterns in customer feedback to prioritize product improvements."
8. "Use regression analysis to understand how changes in product features affect usage."
9. "Develop a churn prediction model to identify at-risk users and why they may leave."
10. "Analyze A/B testing results to determine which variations perform the best."
11. "Measure the impact of pricing changes on sales and user acquisition."
12. "Employ text analytics to derive insights from user reviews and comments."
13. "Create a dashboard for real-time monitoring of key performance indicators (KPIs)."

14. "Forecast inventory needs based on historical sales data and market trends."
15. "Analyze operational data to identify bottlenecks in the product delivery process."
16. "Evaluate customer service interactions to assess impact on customer satisfaction."
17. "Implement machine learning models to personalize user experiences based on behavior."
18. "Conduct sentiment analysis on social media data to gauge brand perception."
19. "Optimize resource allocation using data on team performance and project timelines."
20. "Perform trend analysis to spot emerging patterns in product usage or market conditions."
21. "Analyze competitor data to benchmark and identify areas for competitive advantage."
22. "Use geospatial analysis to understand geographical patterns in user engagement."
23. "Develop models to predict the success of new features based on historical data."
24. "Assess the financial impact of product decisions using revenue and cost analysis."
25. "Utilize data visualization techniques to present complex data in an understandable way."

SECTION 10

SCALING PRODUCTS

Strategies for Scaling Your Product

Scaling a product successfully is a multifaceted endeavor that requires careful planning and strategic execution. As a product gains traction and user base grows, product managers face the challenge of scaling operations to meet increased demand without compromising on quality or user experience. Here are some nuanced strategies to consider when planning to scale a product:

Enhance Technical Infrastructure: As the number of users grows, the strain on your product's infrastructure increases. It's critical to ensure that your servers, databases, and other backend services can handle this increased load. This might involve moving to more robust hosting solutions, utilizing cloud services for better scalability, and implementing efficient data caching mechanisms to improve performance.

Optimize Product Features: Not all features will scale automatically or equally. Identify which features are essential and most used by your growing user base and focus on optimizing these for scalability. This might mean simplifying complex features or enhancing those that offer the most value to ensure they perform efficiently at scale.

Localize and Customize for New Markets: Scaling often involves reaching out to new geographical markets. Each market may have its unique demands and regulatory requirements. Localizing the product in terms of language, cultural nuances, and compliance needs is essential. Moreover, customization might be required to align the product with local market expectations and user preferences.

Expand Operational Capabilities: Scaling your product also means scaling your operations. This includes your supply chain, customer service, and support systems. Ensuring these operations can handle increased volumes without a drop in service quality is crucial. Automating routine tasks and integrating advanced CRM systems can help manage these expanded operations efficiently.

Maintain Quality and Consistency: As you scale, maintaining the quality of your product is paramount. This includes rigorous testing and quality assurance processes to ensure that new updates or features do not compromise the product's integrity. Consistency in user experience across different regions and user segments also needs to be maintained to uphold brand reputation.

Implement Advanced Analytics: Utilize data analytics to monitor how your product is scaling across different dimensions. Advanced tools can help analyze user behavior, feature usage, and system performance in real-time, providing insights that can drive further optimization.

Financial Planning and Management: Scaling operations typically require significant investment. Detailed financial planning is essential to ensure that you can fund the scaling process while maintaining healthy cash flow. This might include budgeting for marketing campaigns, additional staff, new technology, and infrastructure enhancements.

Strengthen Customer Relationships: As your user base grows, maintaining strong customer relationships becomes more challenging but increasingly important. Implement scalable communication strategies, such as segmented email marketing and personalized user engagement campaigns, to keep different user groups engaged and satisfied.

Monitor and Adapt to Market Changes: Market conditions can change rapidly. Regularly monitoring these changes and adapting your strategy accordingly is vital. Stay informed about industry trends, competitor movements, and technological advancements that could impact your scaling strategy.

Foster a Scalable Culture: Scaling a product also involves scaling your team and organizational culture. Foster a culture that embraces change, values innovation, and supports rapid scaling. This includes training your team to handle increased responsibilities and adapting your leadership and management practices to support a larger, more diverse team.

25 AI Prompts for Product Scaling

1. "Analyze infrastructure usage patterns to predict future scalability needs."
2. "Segment user data by geographic region to identify new market opportunities."
3. "Evaluate user engagement across different demographics to tailor scaling strategies."
4. "Forecast demand in new markets based on similar market entry data."
5. "Assess the impact of feature modifications for different user groups."
6. "Optimize customer support resources using predictive demand modeling."
7. "Generate insights into potential regulatory challenges in new markets."

8. "Identify key operational bottlenecks that could hinder scaling efforts."
9. "Simulate the impact of scaling on overall system performance."
10. "Recommend automation processes to streamline operations in scaled scenarios."
11. "Evaluate the effectiveness of current marketing channels in scaled markets."
12. "Analyze competitor scaling strategies to identify best practices and potential pitfalls."
13. "Predict the financial implications of scaling on product profitability."
14. "Assess the cultural nuances in new markets to inform product localization strategies."
15. "Determine the optimal pricing strategy for scaled markets using elasticity analysis."
16. "Recommend partnership opportunities to facilitate smoother scaling."
17. "Develop models to predict customer service needs based on user growth."
18. "Identify features that require scaling based on user feedback and usage data."
19. "Generate risk profiles for entering and expanding in new markets."
20. "Analyze user behavior trends to forecast changes in product requirements."
21. "Propose resource reallocation strategies for optimal scaling."
22. "Evaluate supply chain readiness for increased production demands."
23. "Analyze the scalability of current IT infrastructure under various growth scenarios."
24. "Project changes in user acquisition costs as the product

scales."
25. "Recommend strategies to maintain or improve quality as operations expand."

SECTION 11

PRODUCT LAUNCH AND MARKETING

Effective Product Launch Strategies

Successfully launching a product is a pivotal moment for any business. It requires meticulous planning, strategic marketing, and agile execution to not only introduce the product to the market but also ensure it captures and retains the interest of potential customers. Effective product launch strategies are designed to maximize the impact and visibility of the new product, ensuring a strong market entry and laying the foundation for sustained success.

Deep Market Understanding: Every successful launch begins with a thorough understanding of the market. This involves comprehensive market research to identify potential customers, understand their needs and behaviors, and pinpoint market gaps that the product can fill. It also includes competitive analysis to understand the strengths and weaknesses of similar products in the market. This depth of knowledge ensures that the product meets real user needs and stands out from competitors.

Targeted Messaging and Positioning: Developing clear, compelling messaging that articulates the unique value proposition of the product is crucial. The product's messaging should resonate with the target audience, addressing their specific challenges or desires and explaining how the product can solve them. Effective positioning distinguishes the product from competitors and clarifies why it is the best choice for the target customers.

Strategic Marketing Mix: Utilizing a mix of marketing channels is essential to reach a broad audience. This includes digital channels like social media, email, and online advertising, as well as traditional media such as print, television, and radio, depending on the product and target market. Each channel should be carefully selected and tailored to deliver the product's message effectively to the right audience at the right time.

Optimal Launch Timing: The timing of the product launch can significantly influence its success. Choosing a launch date when target customers are most receptive, and ensuring it does not clash with major industry events or competitor launches, can make a substantial difference. Seasonal trends, market readiness, and company milestones should also be considered to optimize timing.

Dynamic Launch Events: Creating memorable launch events can significantly boost product visibility and engagement. Whether virtual or physical, these events should capture the essence of the product and offer an immersive experience that excites attendees. Engaging key influencers, industry leaders, and media can amplify the launch impact through widespread coverage and social proof.

Promotional Campaigns: Initial promotions, such as discounts, limited-time offers, or exclusive access, can drive early adoption and create buzz around the product. These incentives can encourage users to try the product and provide valuable feedback that can be used to improve the product post-launch.

Feedback and Adaptation: After the launch, it is crucial to monitor the product's performance closely and gather user feedback. This immediate post-launch period is critical for identifying any issues and addressing them swiftly to improve the product and user experience. Adapting marketing strategies based on user engagement and feedback can also help sustain momentum after the initial launch.

Post-Launch Support and Engagement: Maintaining high levels of customer support and engagement after the launch is vital for retaining early adopters and converting them into long-term customers. This includes responsive customer service, ongoing communication through updates and newsletters, and continuous enhancement of the product based on user needs and technological advancements.

25 AI Prompts for Product Launch and Marketing

1. "Generate a comprehensive competitor analysis for [product name] prior to launch."
2. "Create a series of press releases for different stages of the product launch."
3. "Develop a targeted social media campaign plan for [product name]."
4. "Simulate potential customer responses to the product launch using sentiment analysis."
5. "Produce a list of key influencers in [industry] to target for [product name] promotion."
6. "Design an email marketing strategy for engaging potential customers pre-launch."
7. "Forecast sales figures for [product name] in the first quarter post-launch."
8. "Identify the most effective promotional channels for [product name] based on target demographics."
9. "Create engaging blog content outlines to support the product launch."
10. "Develop a crisis management strategy for potential issues during the product launch."
11. "Analyze past launch data to identify successful tactics for [product category]."

12. "Generate SEO keywords to optimize online content for the product launch."
13. "Design a post-launch survey to collect customer feedback on [product name]."
14. "Create a virtual launch event plan, including agenda and guest speakers."
15. "Simulate the impact of different discount strategies on initial sales volume."
16. "Develop FAQs for customer service to address anticipated inquiries post-launch."
17. "Generate a digital advertising plan with budget allocation and expected ROI."
18. "Plan a series of webinars to demonstrate the features of [product name]."
19. "Create a media kit for [product name] including product photos, descriptions, and user benefits."
20. "Design banner ads for display on targeted online platforms."
21. "Generate a timeline for phased rollout of [product name] in multiple markets."
22. "Develop a content marketing calendar focusing on the benefits of [product name]."
23. "Analyze the effectiveness of past product launches to improve current strategies."
24. "Create promotional video concepts that highlight the unique features of [product name]."
25. "Develop a post-launch analysis report template to evaluate marketing effectiveness and product reception."

SECTION 12

LEADERSHIP AND STAKEHOLDER MANAGEMENT

Managing Teams and Stakeholders

Effective management of teams and stakeholders is pivotal for the success of any product initiative. Product managers must navigate complex interpersonal dynamics and ensure clear communication to drive product development forward. This task involves not only leading teams with clarity and empathy but also managing relationships with various stakeholders who influence or are impacted by the product.

Team Management

The cornerstone of successful team management is fostering a collaborative environment where each team member feels valued and empowered. Product managers must ensure that team roles are clearly defined and that every member understands how their contributions fit into the larger product vision. This clarity helps in minimizing confusion and aligning efforts towards common goals.

Creating an open communication culture is critical. Team members should feel comfortable sharing their ideas, concerns, and feedback. Regular meetings, such as daily stand-ups or weekly check-ins, facilitate ongoing communication and help keep everyone on the same page. These interactions also provide opportunities for team members to report on their progress, discuss challenges, and collaboratively seek solutions.

Motivation and engagement are fueled by recognition and growth opportunities. Product managers should regularly acknowledge individual and team achievements, providing positive reinforcement that boosts morale and productivity. Additionally, supporting professional development and career advancement for team members not only enhances their skills but also contributes to their long-term engagement and loyalty.

Stakeholder Management

Stakeholder management requires a strategic approach to communicating and collaborating with all parties interested in or affected by the product. Stakeholders can include internal teams, such as executives and cross-functional partners, as well as external entities like customers, suppliers, and regulatory bodies.

Understanding the expectations, concerns, and objectives of each stakeholder group is the first step in effective stakeholder management. Product managers should conduct regular meetings with stakeholders to gather insights and keep them informed of project progress. These interactions help in building trust and ensuring that stakeholder needs are considered in decision-making processes.

Effective communication is tailored and transparent. Product managers must craft messages that are clear and relevant to the interests of each stakeholder group. This might involve adjusting the level of detail, the complexity of information, and the method of communication to suit the specific audience. For instance, technical details may be crucial for engineering teams but not for sales teams or customers.

Managing stakeholder relationships also involves negotiation and conflict resolution. Product managers must be skilled in navigating disagreements and aligning diverse interests without compromising the product's objectives or quality. This often requires a balance of diplomacy, firmness, and compromise.

Integrating Team and Stakeholder Management

Integrating effective team and stakeholder management practices requires a balance of leadership skills and interpersonal savvy. Product managers act as the linchpin, aligning team efforts with stakeholder expectations and guiding the product journey through various challenges and milestones.

By fostering a positive, transparent, and proactive management style, product managers can cultivate a productive work environment and build robust relationships that propel product success. This approach not only accelerates product development but also enhances team and stakeholder satisfaction, laying a strong foundation for current and future projects.

25 AI Prompts for Leadership and Stakeholder Engagement

1. "Generate a list of key leadership traits most valued in our industry and assess current team leaders against these traits."
2. "Develop a customized leadership development program for emerging leaders within the product management team."
3. "Create a stakeholder mapping and engagement strategy for our upcoming product launch."
4. "Simulate potential stakeholder reactions to major project updates and prepare mitigation strategies."
5. "Analyze communication effectiveness between cross-functional teams and provide recommendations for improvement."
6. "Design a feedback mechanism that allows team members to anonymously share their thoughts on leadership effectiveness."

7. "Develop a series of conflict resolution scenarios and training materials tailored to common challenges in our projects."
8. "Generate a guide on effective virtual communication strategies for managing distributed teams."
9. "Create a decision-making framework that includes input from all relevant stakeholders to ensure balanced and fair outcomes."
10. "Assess the impact of recent leadership decisions on team morale and productivity."
11. "Recommend strategies to enhance transparency and trust between the management team and other employees."
12. "Develop a quarterly review template focused on leadership performance and stakeholder satisfaction."
13. "Generate an onboarding plan for new stakeholders to quickly bring them up to speed on project objectives and status."
14. "Create a crisis management playbook tailored to potential risks in our product development cycles."
15. "Analyze past project failures to identify leadership and stakeholder management shortcomings."
16. "Develop a plan for regular leadership and stakeholder engagement workshops."
17. "Generate a template for a leadership dashboard that tracks key performance indicators related to team management and stakeholder engagement."
18. "Create a risk assessment report for stakeholder pushback on new product features and propose communication strategies to address concerns."
19. "Simulate the impact of changes in project scope on stakeholder expectations and suggest adjustments in communication strategy."
20. "Develop guidelines for proactive versus reactive

communication strategies in stakeholder management."
21. "Generate a list of motivational tactics that can be employed by leaders during challenging phases of product development."
22. "Create a strategy for managing upward communication to keep upper management informed and engaged in key project decisions."
23. "Develop a plan for integrating stakeholder feedback into the product development process without derailing the project timeline."
24. "Generate a series of email templates for communicating bad news to stakeholders in a way that maintains trust and confidence."
25. "Create a comprehensive guide for newly appointed product managers on managing teams and stakeholders effectively."

CONCLUSION

Throughout this book, we've explored the transformative impact of artificial intelligence on product management, demonstrating how AI can significantly enhance the effectiveness and efficiency of product development. As we have seen, AI's capacity to automate routine tasks, generate deep insights from large data sets, and predict future trends allows product managers to make more informed decisions, tailor products to meet specific customer needs, and swiftly adapt to changing market dynamics.

The integration of AI tools throughout the product lifecycle—from initial market analysis and customer feedback interpretation to risk management and strategic scaling—has not only streamlined operations but also opened new avenues for innovation. This technological evolution challenges product managers to continually refine their skills and expand their understanding of AI's capabilities to fully leverage these tools in driving product success.

Looking forward, the role of AI in product management is set to grow, marked by advances in predictive analytics, machine learning, and intelligent automation. This progression will necessitate a balance between leveraging technological advancements and maintaining ethical standards, as transparency, privacy, and unbiased decision-making remain paramount.

Moreover, as AI becomes more embedded in our everyday processes, the boundary between technology and human oversight will increasingly blur, making it crucial for product managers to keep the human element central in their strategies. This involves designing products that are not only technically sound but also ethically responsible and aligned with human values.

In conclusion, the journey through AI-enhanced product management is one of ongoing learning and adaptation. For product managers, the future is not just about managing products but about leading with innovation, foresight, and responsibility, ensuring that products not only succeed in the market but also contribute positively to the society in which they are used. Embracing AI with awareness and intention will be key to shaping a future where technology and humanity progress together.

ABOUT THE AUTHOR

Ethan Dawn Harper is a seasoned professional with a rich academic and industry background in communication technologies and information technology. Holding a Ph.D. in communication technologies, Ethan has spent over a decade in the IT field, contributing in various capacities ranging from product quality to delivery, development, and management.

His extensive experience spans both the academic and practical aspects of technology, providing him with a unique perspective that he brings to his current endeavors. Ethan's deep understanding of the complexities of product management in IT, combined with his academic insights, makes him a respected figure in his field.

www.ingramcontent.com/pod-product-compliance
Lightning Source LLC
Chambersburg PA
CBHW070359230526
45471CB00006B/2646